LIVING GREEN

Green Buildings

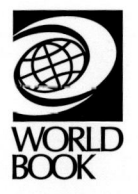

WORLD
BOOK

a Scott Fetzer company

Chicago

www.worldbookonline.com

Editorial:

Editor in Chief: Paul A. Kobasa
Project Manager: Cassie Mayer
Writer: Robert N. Knight
Editor: Brian Johnson
Researchers: Michael Barr, Cheryl Graham
*Manager, Contracts & Compliance
  (Rights & Permissions):* Loranne K. Shields
Indexer: David Pofelski

Graphics and Design:

Associate Director: Sandra M. Dyrlund
Associate Manager, Design: Brenda B. Tropinski
Associate Manager, Photography: Tom Evans
Book design by: Don Di Sante
Senior Cartographer: John Rejba

Pre-Press and Manufacturing:

Director: Carma Fazio
Manufacturing Manager: Steve Hueppchen
Production/Technology Manager: Anne Fritzinger

World Book, Inc.
233 N. Michigan Avenue
Chicago, IL 60601
U.S.A.

For information about other World Book publications, visit our Web site at **http://www.worldbookonline.com** or call **1-800-WORLDBK (967-5325).**

For information about sales to schools and libraries, call **1-800-975-3250 (United States),** or **1-800-837-5365 (Canada).**

Library of Congress Cataloging-in-Publication Data

Green buildings.
   p. cm. -- (Living green)
  Includes index.
  Summary: "An exploration of green architectural principals and practices. Features include fact boxes, sidebars, activities, glossary, list of recommended reading and Web sites, and index"--Provided by publisher.
   ISBN 978-0-7166-1404-3
   1. Sustainable buildings--Juvenile literature. 2. Sustainable living--Juvenile literature. 3. Energy conservation--Juvenile literature. I. World Book, Inc.
 TH880.G7425 2009
 720'.47--dc22
                    2008035509

Picture Acknowledgments:

Front Cover: © David Hoffman Photo Library/Alamy Images

© Ace Stock/Alamy Images 23; © Thomas A. Heinz, Arcaid/Alamy Images 25; © Morey Milbradt, Jupiter Images/Brand X/Alamy Images 7; © brt photo/Alamy Images 9; © Jupiterimages/Comstock/Alamy Images 59; © John Walmsley, Education Photos/Alamy Images 39; © Falkensteinfoto/Alamy Images 45; © David Frazier Photolibrary/Alamy Images 15; © Jeff Greenberg, Alamy Images 7; © David Hancock, Alamy Images 54; © Norbert Michalke, imagebroker/Alamy Images 40; © Les Ladbury, Alamy Images 55; © Lou Linwei, Alamy Images 27; © Iain Masterton, Alamy Images 5; © Richard Mittleman, Alamy Images 42; © Jeff Morgan Alternative Technology/Alamy Images 54; © Nic Miller, Organics Image Library/Alamy Images 1; © Chris Rose, PropertyStock/Alamy Images 16; © Frances Roberts, Alamy Images 31; © Jay Sturdevant, Alamy Images 55; © Elizabeth Whiting, Alamy Images 14; © XenGate/Alamy Images 18; © Addison Doty, American Clay Ent. 19; © Martin Bond from Peter Arnold, Inc. 6, 57; © Paul Glendell from Peter Arnold, Inc. 38; © Buro North 34; © California Academy of Sciences 31; City of Melbourne 43, 50, 51; © Saxon Holt, PhotoBotanic/Digital Railroad 47; © Peter Aaron, Esto 52; © Sarah Leen, National Geographic/Getty Images 33; © KieranTimberlake Associates 53; Kirei USA 11; © Masterfile 56; © Brad Wrobleski, Masterfile 24; National Renewable Energy Laboratory 26, 29, 30, 43; Jim Parodi Wallpapering (www.parodipalace.com) 21; © Shutterstock 8, 10, 12, 13, 14, 20, 22, 27, 28, 32, 35, 36, 37, 39, 45, 49, 58; Society for Editors and Proofreaders 46; © Digital Vision/SuperStock 8; © image100/SuperStock 48; © Photographers Choice RF/SuperStock 4; © Tyler A. Walter 17.

All maps and illustrations are the exclusive property of World Book, Inc.

Living Green
Set ISBN: 978-0-7166-1400-5
Printed in Mexico
1 2 3 4 5 12 11 10 09 08

Table of Contents

There is a glossary of terms on pages 60-61. Terms defined in the glossary are in type **that looks like this** on their first appearance in any section.

What Is Green Architecture?

Today, there's a new buzzword in our society: green. "Green" or "Earth-friendly" describes a way of living and thinking that takes into account the health of planet Earth and embraces limits on our use of resources. Not long ago, green was not fashionable. Consumers wanted bigger, more powerful cars, energy-intensive air conditioners and heaters in their homes and offices, and all the other "goodies" provided by modern industrial civilization. But today, a green attitude is becoming popular in movies and magazines, and the world's most talented designers are going green.

Many of today's architects, the professionals who design buildings, are using their creative talent and knowledge of technology to design attractive buildings that are Earth-friendly. Green buildings reduce consumption of energy, water, and other natural resources. They incorporate **renewable resources**, which can be grown as crops or gathered from the environment without danger of running out. The ultimate goal of green architecture is **sustainability**, or functioning in complete harmony with the natural environment.

Why we need green architecture

Earth is home to more than 6 billion people, and populations continue to grow. Many experts fear that we are using natural resources too rapidly to be sustained. Supplies of energy resources and water are especially threatened. Moreover, we are using these resources in ways that pollute and otherwise harm Earth.

Buildings use a lion's share of energy resources. In fact, more than 40 percent of the world's energy goes into operating buildings. Buildings also use great quantities of treated water—that is, water that has been purified in a water treatment plant. Moving toward sustainability will require a complete turnaround in the construction industry. That's where green architecture comes in.

The energy supply

For the past century or more, much of the world has run on the energy in **petroleum** (also called oil), coal, and natural gas—the fuels known as **fossil fuels**. Fossil fuels come from underground deposits that were formed millions of years ago from the remains of plants and animals. Today, we know that supplies of fossil fuels are dwindling and will eventually run out. Thus, they are called **nonrenewable resources**.

Fossil fuels must be burned to use their energy, which releases the gas **carbon dioxide**. Carbon dioxide is a key part of Earth's **atmosphere** because it helps **regulate** (control) the temperature by retaining some of the sun's heat. This process is called the **greenhouse effect**. Carbon dioxide and other gases that trap the sun's heat are called **greenhouse gases**. As we burn fossil fuels and put more carbon dioxide into the atmosphere, more and more heat is trapped.

Global warming

Growing levels of carbon dioxide have caused **global warming**. Scientists have shown that the air temperature of Earth has been rising gradually for decades, and nearly all scientists believe that rising temperatures are caused by human activities—especially burning fossil fuels. People around the world have begun to tackle the problem of global warming. In order to reduce global warming, we must change the way we construct and renovate buildings.

The greenhouse effect traps more energy from the sun, raising global temperatures. Many human activities release greenhouse gases into the atmosphere.

Taking advantage of cool breezes from lakes (top) and installing "green roofs" (bottom) are two ways to make buildings more energy efficient.

Passive design

The fundamental principle of the green architecture movement is passive design. Passive design calls for buildings that make the best use of such natural elements as sunlight, wind, vegetation, and rainwater to substantially reduce "active" consumption of energy and other resources.

For example, suppose an architect is designing a building that will be constructed on the shore of a bay that regularly produces cool breezes in the afternoon. For the architect, this natural wind pattern presents an ideal opportunity to use such breezes to reduce the building's need for artificial cooling. The architect's design could include bayside windows that open automatically in the afternoon, allowing cool breezes to flow into the building. While electrical air conditioning might be needed at times, the energy needed to cool the building will be much lower than it would be otherwise.

An example of such a building is Queenscliffe Centre, a research facility on the coast of the state of Victoria, in Australia. The building is a long, narrow structure on a finger of land that is surrounded by water. It is in an ideal position for capturing bay breezes that can flow through the interior. In another ingenious use of the natural environment, architects designed a cooling system for Queenscliffe Centre that uses cool seawater channeled through pipes in the building. This exceptionally green building illustrates the principle of passive design in many other ways as well.

The climate factor

Climate greatly impacts green design. For example, cooling by natural **ventilation** works better in dry climates than in humid

climates. Humidity makes hot air difficult to tolerate. Humidity must be removed from the air inside most buildings, but it is often removed in an energy-intensive way.

Adobe buildings stay cool in the daytime but give off heat at night.

The need to heat a building adequately in a climate with cold winters usually requires burning some fossil fuels. However, using efficient, high-tech natural gas furnaces can reduce energy consumption and carbon-dioxide emissions.

In climates with cold but sunny winters, heat provided by sunlight can reduce the need to burn fossil fuels. Native Americans of the American Southwest have long used principles of passive design to construct their adobe houses. Adobe is a type of sun-dried brick made by mixing clay, sand, and water. This mixture is shaped and left to dry in a wooden form. The bricks are then removed from the form and dried further in the sun for about a month.

Adobe bricks create thick, massive walls that change temperature very slowly. In a climate with sunny winters, this is a great advantage. During daytime, the adobe walls slowly absorb warmth from winter sunlight. When temperatures fall sharply at night, the adobe gives off its stored heat, reducing the amount of fuel needed for heaters. The heating and cooling capacity of adobe illustrates yet another beneficial use of passive design.

In downtown Phoenix, Arizona, high-rise owners cool their buildings with a shared system called Northwind Phoenix. Three million pounds of ice are stored underground at night. Then, as the ice melts during the day, cold water runs through pipes connected to the buildings and cools them just as conventional air conditioning would. The water is continually recycled when each night a cheap, low-impact form of refrigeration refreezes it.

Arizona high-rises

Building Materials

Section Summary

Building materials often require much energy to manufacture. They also affect how much energy is used to keep buildings at a comfortable temperature.

Green building materials may require less energy to produce. They also may help to make the building more energy efficient and create a healthy living or working environment.

Responsible architects and builders choose construction materials carefully. For each material, they consider the following three issues:

- The amount of energy required to process or manufacture the material and transport it.
- How safe the material will be for people who will use the finished building.
- How the material will affect energy use in the building.

Embodied energy

The amount of energy used to produce and transport construction materials is called **embodied energy**. Measuring a material's embodied energy is difficult, but some guidelines are helpful. Materials that require great heat and pressure to produce, such as metals, require large amounts of energy. Shipping heavy materials long distances requires much energy, too. Materials in both of these examples have high embodied energy. By contrast, locally obtained natural materials that require little processing have low

Producing metals typically requires large amounts of energy.

embodied energy. Using energy wisely is a major focus of any green activity.

Material safety

Government agencies and the construction industry monitor the safety of materials. However, the possibility that a manufactured product could be harmful still exists.

One issue of great concern is the **volatile organic compounds (VOC's)** found in many manufactured products—especially certain glues, sealers, paints, solvents (chemicals used to keep substances liquid), and plastics. Among the most dangerous VOC's are chemicals that come from **petroleum.** VOC's break down over time and give off small amounts of toxic gases. Green builders look for ways to replace materials that give off VOC's with natural products.

Energy-smart materials

Many green builders use materials that will help a building stay cool in summer and warm in winter. These materials, such as adobe brick, often have high **thermal mass.** That is, they slowly change temperature, helping to **regulate** the interior temperature of the building. Such materials can help keep temperatures away from cold and hot extremes. They reduce the need for artificial heating and cooling, which require much energy.

Non-green building materials

Most buildings today are constructed from materials that are not considered green. For example, many manufactured building materials contain petroleum. They include **vinyl** flooring and wallpaper, glues, caulking compounds (materials used to fill in gaps where air is leaking), paints, stains, and other products. Petroleum is a **nonrenewable resource** that is used for many human activities. It is burned for energy in vehicles and at factories and power plants.

Building materials can harm the environment in many ways. They often take much energy to manufacture, which leads to higher levels of pollution. They may also cause additional environmental pollution when they are discarded.

Many building materials, such as vinyl flooring, are made from petroleum, a nonrenewable resource.

Synthetic materials

Some **synthetic materials** (manufactured materials that do not exist in nature) do not **biodegrade,** or break down easily in nature. When such materials are discarded, they usually go into **landfills,** which can leak toxic liquids and gases. Synthetic materials that are not biodegradable are mainly plastics. PVC is a type of plastic that is often used to make pipes. Teflon is a type of plastic that is used for insulating.

Some materials that do not biodegrade can be recycled for other uses. For example, some nonbiodegradable plastics can be chopped into fine pieces and used as filler in products or in packaging.

Plumbing pipes are often made of PVC, a plastic material that is not biodegradable.

Heavy metals

Such metals as lead, mercury, and cadmium are called **heavy metals.** These metals are harmful to humans and other animals in a variety of ways, and even small amounts can be dangerous. For example, in the past, many pipes used in plumbing were made of lead. Hot water moving through lead pipes can dissolve some of the lead. This dissolved lead poses a danger to people who drink the water. Lead was also used for many years as an ingredient in house paints. When these paints age, crack, and peel, they sometimes flake off walls. Small children may pick up the flakes and put them in their mouths, putting them at risk for severe health problems.

For these reasons, it is wise to eliminate heavy metals entirely from all construction materials. Today, plumbing materials and paints that do not contain lead are widely available.

Green building materials

What makes some construction materials greener than others? Green materials can be harvested and used without polluting, without consuming large amounts of energy, and without depleting Earth's natural resources. Using our planet's resources wisely is ever more important as our population grows.

Today, architects are increasingly using **renewable resources** as building materials. Some of these materials are rapidly renewable. For example, manufacturers make a construction material called Kirei Board that is made from sorghum stalks. Sorghum is a food crop that can be grown in a single season.

Recycled materials

Many "non-green" building materials have properties that make them ideal for building construction. Because of this, they will likely continue to be used by architects, at least for the near future. However, there are several ways to reduce a building material's environmental impact. Old materials can be recycled, or processed for reuse. For example, materials used in a building's construction, such as wall and roof insulation, are sometimes made from recycled content. Wall board, a common finish for walls, can also be recycled.

Reclaimed materials

Saving old materials for reuse in a similar way is called **reclaiming** or **salvaging**. Today, many demolition companies allow salvaging companies to remove materials from buildings before they are destroyed. Such materials might include woodwork, mantels, wood flooring, doors, stained-glass windows, and other items. Many people are eager to use such materials in new houses or other buildings. Salvaging materials does not disturb the natural environment, and it consumes only the energy required for salvage and transportation.

Choosing building materials

Determining a building material's overall environmental impact can be difficult. For example, some materials may have a high embodied energy, but they may also have a high thermal mass, helping to reduce a building's energy use. The following pages consider the environmental impact of common building materials.

Kirei Board, used to make this table, is an eco-friendly material for furniture and flooring.

Wood

Traditionally, people have use wood for the frames of homes and for such interior elements as floors, doors, window frames, molding, and fireplace mantels. However, irresponsible logging has led to **deforestation**, wiping out entire forests in some areas. Trees are a renewable resource, but they are not rapidly renewable. Hardwood trees, such as maple, oak, and cherry, require 90 to 100 years or more to reach maturity.

Forests play a key role in Earth's ecology. Living plants absorb carbon dioxide and give off oxygen. By absorbing carbon dioxide, forests slow **global warming**.

Building frames for homes are commonly made from wood, a natural resource that takes many years to regrow.

One alternative to cutting down hardwood trees is using reclaimed wood. As communities change and grow, some old buildings are demolished. Many old buildings contain hardwood harvested long ago. Using reclaimed wood yields many benefits. No new trees are cut. The energy that would have been consumed logging and transporting new wood is saved. Also, reusing old materials keeps them out of landfills.

Steel

Steel is a strong material that is made from iron and the chemical element carbon. It is used in the construction of many large buildings, such as skyscrapers. However, steel does have some environmental drawbacks. The iron in steel must be mined from the ground, a process that can cause environmental damage. Steel production requires very high heat, so steel also has high embodied energy. Coal is burned to produce this high heat, which releases **greenhouse gases** into the **atmosphere**.

Steel's strength and durability make it a desirable building material for many architects. However, some green architects have sought to reduce steel's environmental impact by using reclaimed or recycled steel.

Concrete

Concrete has high embodied energy.

Like steel, concrete is an incredibly strong material that is used to build the foundation of many buildings. It is made from a mixture of water, portland cement, and aggregates. Portland cement is a fine gray powder made from a specific mixture of minerals. Aggregates are such materials as sand, gravel, and crushed rock.

Concrete has high embodied energy. Aggregates and ingredients in portland cement must be mined, which is energy-intensive. Manufacturing portland cement requires high heat and pressure, which requires even more energy.

Concrete has some green qualities. A thick concrete floor has high thermal mass. Floors and walls that can hold heat reduce the need for artificial heating and cooling.

Some green builders use concrete that is made partly from recycled ingredients. Fly ash, a residue from burning coal, can substitute for some of the portland cement.

Flooring

Section Summary

Flooring is the general name given to all materials used to cover floors. When it comes to flooring, green architects consider two main things: how the production of the material affects the environment, and how the material will affect energy use in the building.

Green builders often use natural materials for flooring. These include wood from forests that have been managed responsibly, reclaimed wood from demolished buildings, and plant materials that can be grown rapidly.

Today, many people have switched to sustainable flooring materials, including cork.

Depending on the type of building, floors must support the weight of furniture, home appliances, office equipment, storage units, merchandise (goods for sale), and other objects. Flooring must also provide stable surfaces on which people can walk. The type and quality of flooring can affect energy use. For example, a thin, uninsulated floor in an unheated room could draw away heat from inhabited, heated rooms below, increasing energy costs in winter.

Wood floors

Traditionally, wood is the most common flooring material. Hardwood floors are natural, beautiful, and long-lasting, but using hardwood can contribute to **deforestation**. However, not all logging is environmentally destructive. Builders can confirm that wood products have been harvested in an environmentally responsible way by using wood that has been **certified** by the Forest Stewardship Council (FSC). (For more information on the FSC, see the "Closer Look" sidebar on page 13.)

Cork flooring

In recent years, cork has become a popular material for green flooring. Cork is the bark of a tree that grows in countries around the Mediterranean Sea. Cork is slightly spongy. It is often used for bulletin boards, for example, because thumbtacks can easily pierce cork. Many people like cork floors because they give a little underneath your feet.

Cork bark can be harvested from cork oak trees once every 10 years without harming the trees, so cork is considered renewable. Cork flooring usually comes in rolls or tiles. It is attached to a base floor with glue. Then, a finish, such as wax or a sealing chemical, is applied to the surface to protect the cork. To achieve a truly green cork floor, builders should use natural glue and waxes that do not contain **volatile organic compounds (VOC's).**

Bamboo flooring

Bamboo is a type of grass that is native to East Asia. It grows very rapidly and becomes quite tall. Unlike most grasses, bamboo grows as tough, hollow canes. Strips of bamboo cane can be used to make durable, attractive wood floors that resemble hardwood floors.

Because it grows so fast, bamboo is a highly **renewable resource.** New sprouts become full-grown in about five years. Properly managed bamboo plantings could supply much of the market for "hardwood" floors.

Reclaimed wood

An attractive alternative to using new hardwood for flooring is using **reclaimed** wood. Most reclaimed wood comes from old buildings that are demolished. The interiors of many old buildings contain high-quality hardwood that was harvested many years ago. Reclaimed wood is attractive and very much in fashion.

Resanding old floors can make them look new again.

Stone floors have high thermal mass, reducing the need for heating and cooling.

Linoleum floors

Linoleum is a type of flooring often used in kitchens and bathrooms. People sometimes refer to any water-resistant flooring surface as "linoleum." However, true linoleum is made from linseed oil, sawdust, cork dust, pine resin (sap), powdered chalk, and dyes, all of which are mixed and pressed onto a backing of burlap, a heavy cloth. Linoleum is a greener product than **vinyl** flooring, which is sometimes mistakenly called linoleum. All the ingredients in linoleum are recyclable. Vinyl flooring, on the other hand, is manufactured from **petroleum** in an energy-intensive process. It is not easily recycled. Vinyl also gives off volatile organic compounds.

Stone and concrete floors

Some green architects choose stone or concrete floors to increase a home's energy efficiency. A thick stone or concrete floor has high **thermal mass**, which helps reduce the need for artificial heating and cooling. Water pipes can be installed under or through such a floor. The floor's thermal mass holds and distributes heat from hot water in winter. In summer, cool water draws heat out of the floor, reducing the room's temperature. (For more information on **radiant heating and cooling**, see page 42).

Earthen floors

Today, homeowners can enjoy all the comforts of home on a special kind of earthen floor. These floors are made of mud mixed with other ingredients. The earthen floor is specially constructed and finished so as to have a solid, clean surface.

The first step to making an earthen floor is mixing mud with sand, lime, and straw or other fibrous material in just the right proportions. This mud mixture is spread thickly and evenly over a subfloor. It is smoothed out and allowed to dry for one to two weeks. Then, the earthen floor is ready for a final step: sealing the surface with linseed oil and beeswax. These sealants protect the floor and give it a warm, beautiful shine. Some people think finished earthen floors look like leather.

You may imagine that earthen floors could throw dust into the air, or that mopping them could create a muddy mess. However, the oils and waxes that are applied to earthen floors keep them from spreading dust and give them a solid, washable surface.

Earthen floors help rooms stay warm in winter and cool in summer. The thick, dense layer of soil has high thermal mass. The floor changes temperature very slowly. In winter, sunlight coming through a window warms the earthen floor. The heated floor then gives off heat at night. In summer, the earthen floor becomes cool at night and absorbs heat during hot days.

GREEN FACT

Linoleum was a popular choice for flooring during the late 1800's and early 1900's, until vinyl sheeting came along in the 1940's. Oddly, it was the durability of linoleum that contributed much to its decline. Linoleum lasts 40 years or more—about twice as long as vinyl—and people simply got tired of having it around so long.

Earthen Floor—Advantages and Disadvantages	
Advantages	**Disadvantages**
Has high thermal mass, good for heating and cooling	Can crack, especially if floor ingredients are not mixed in the proper proportion
Has very low embodied energy: 90 percent less than finished concrete	Surface can get scratched up
Less expensive than a hardwood floor	May be hard to find a contractor with knowledge and skills needed to build an earthen floor
Attractive surface with the look and feel of leather	Not appropriate for very high traffic areas, such as hallways
Has no VOC's, gives off no pollution	Not appropriate for wet areas, such as kitchens and bathrooms
Floor gives slightly; comfortable to walk on	Pointy chair legs or high-heel shoes can dent floor surface
Uses natural ingredients	
Eliminates construction waste; "leftovers" can be recycled	

Some people install earthen floors themselves or with the help of friends.

Walls

Section Summary

Walls are made from a variety of materials. To build green, it is important to use Earth-friendly, nontoxic materials to construct, cover, and decorate walls. Traditional materials often require large amounts of energy to manufacture. Many include substances that can pollute the environment when they are thrown out.

Natural materials for building and covering walls are gaining popularity. They require less energy to make and include few harmful chemicals. Some standard materials for walls are also being reused and recycled to reduce their environmental impact.

The construction of walls often involves nailing drywall sheets over a wood frame.

Within a building, interior walls often account for more surface area than either floors or ceilings. To build green, it is important to use Earth-friendly, nontoxic materials to construct, cover, and decorate walls.

How walls are made

There are many ways to construct interior walls. However, the most common method is to build a frame by nailing together long pieces of sawed wood. **Drywall** sheets are then nailed over the frame. Drywall sheets, also called wallboard, are made of a mineral called gypsum that is backed with paper.

Some walls are finished by applying plaster to make them airtight and to provide a finished surface. Standard plaster is made by mixing sand, gypsum or portland cement, and water. Plaster is safe for interiors where people will live and work. However, it requires large amounts of energy to manufacture. Gypsum must be mined. Then, it must be heated to a high temperature and crushed. These processes are energy-intensive. Manufacturing portland cement is also very energy-intensive.

Earth plaster

Many green-thinking builders are now using earth plaster for house interiors. Earth plaster is made by substituting natural clay for the gypsum or portland cement in standard plaster. The clay must be dug out of the ground, but it does not have to be heated and has low **embodied energy**.

Earth plaster gives interior walls a natural look. Typically, the plaster shows some texture instead of being smooth, like standard plaster. The clays and pigments (coloring agents) used in earth plaster yield warm earth tones.

Many people find earth plaster walls appealing, but this finishing material does have some drawbacks. It is easier to scratch or crack earth plaster than standard plaster. Also, its color may vary from one batch to another.

Drywall

In many parts of the world, drywall is the most commonly used material for the construction of interior walls. Typically, about 12 percent of new drywall is wasted during construction, due mainly to cutting the drywall sheets to fit. This waste amounts to more than a ton of material from the construction of one medium-sized house.

Although drywall itself isn't particularly toxic, drywall waste can create problems. Gypsum, the main ingredient in drywall, contains the minerals calcium and sulfur. In **landfills**, sulfur can break down and form hydrogen sulfide, a toxic gas.

Drywall is considered a very useful building material, so its use is not likely to be phased out any time soon. Many industry experts say that expanding efforts to recycle waste drywall can help reduce its environmental impact. The gypsum in waste drywall can be ground up and formed into new drywall. However, the paper backing must first be removed from the drywall, which makes the process less efficient than the recycling of other types of materials. Recycling companies are still searching for ways to improve drywall waste recycling.

Reusing drywall is perhaps the easiest way to reduce its environmental impact. The gypsum in drywall can improve some kinds of soil. For this reason, ground-up drywall is added to soil in many places. Cement factories can also use the gypsum recovered from scrap drywall. However, the paper content must be less than 1 percent.

Some waste-conscious builders use another method to dispose of drywall scraps. They put them in the spaces in walls between the inside and outside surfaces to act as **insulation.**

Earth plaster, which was used to cover these walls, has lower embodied energy than traditional plaster.

Paint in the world of green

Nothing can brighten up a room so much as a fresh coat of paint. But a new coat of paint can cost more than the price of paint and labor. It can cause headaches, burning eyes, and other reactions. Many paints manufactured and sold for use in homes, offices, and schools contain formaldehyde and other **volatile organic compounds (VOC's).** Some types of wet paint can give off VOC's at a level 1,000 times the normal outdoor level of these chemicals.

The paint disposal problem

In addition to posing risks for people living and working in painted areas, paint poses a serious disposal problem. According to a recent study, the average U.S. household stockpiles 1 to 3 gallons (4 to 11 liters) of paint per year. This is mainly because it is hard to estimate the exact amount of paint required for a job, so people usually overstock. Then, they must either store the extra paint or discard it.

Most states have strict rules for paint disposal. Cans of partly used paint must be discarded at special recycling centers instead of in the regular trash. Paint should never be poured down storm sewers. Some home improvement experts advise people to buy only as much paint as they think they will need. They can use any excess paint to apply additional coats.

Traditional paints give off formaldehyde and other VOC's as they dry.

Recycled paints

Some paint manufacturers make recycled or reblended paint products from unused paint. Recycled paints are medium-cost, high-quality products that come in a wide variety of colors. Reblended paints are less-expensive, lower-quality products that come in only a few colors.

Natural paints

Today, green manufacturers are making paints that use natural ingredients and have minimal or no VOC's or other toxic ingredients. One category of such paints is clay-based paints. These paints are comparable to standard paints in quality. They also have no odor and they are easy to clean up. However, some industry observers claim that they are not as sturdy or durable as standard paints.

Another category of natural paints is milk-based paints. The basic ingredient in these paints is casein, a protein in milk. A milk-paint finish must be sealed with a hard finish. The milk paint also must be used quickly, because in wet form, it may become spoiled by mold.

Earth-friendly wallpaper

A popular alternative to painting interior walls is wallpapering them. Wallpaper has been around for centuries. During the mid-1900's, however, manufacturers changed their formulas to incorporate **synthetic materials** into papers. They also replaced natural inks and glues with synthetic ones, which are toxic. As a result, many wallpaper products give off harmful VOC's.

The trend today has returned toward natural papers, inks, and glues. Builders who want natural wallpaper products can find them. Natural wallpaper contributes to a safer, more wholesome living or working environment. Moreover, discarded natural wallpaper can be **composted,** or piled up in masses where it eventually breaks down into natural **fertilizer.**

Natural grass cloths are becoming popular again, too. Manufacturers make these attractive wall coverings by weaving together such plant material as grass, bamboo, jute, sisal, or hemp. They can be hung just like regular wallpaper.

Some home improvement experts publish recipes for making homemade wallpaper paste. These recipes use flour, water, alum (a natural chemical salt), and small amounts of other ingredients. It is easy to find wallpaper paste recipes on the Internet.

Natural wallpaper uses no synthetics in the paper or in the glue that holds it in place.

Doors

Section Summary

Doors can affect the energy use of a building. For example, if doors allow heat to escape from a home in winter, more energy is required to heat the building. Doors can also let in air through cracks and gaps around a door-frame.

Many doors are made of wood. Wood that comes from well-managed forests or re-claimed wood are two environ-mentally friendly options for doors. Some doors are made from a mixture of materials that provide good insulation. How-ever, these materials require much energy to manufacture and may give off toxic gases.

Doors often allow large heat gain or loss from a building, even when they are closed.

The front door is a building's gateway to the outside world. It is also a point of large heat gain or loss. This is an especially important issue in areas with bitterly cold winters, because heating buildings during intense cold requires large amounts of energy, and cold, dense air quickly invades the interior of a heated building.

Maintaining a tight barrier

Heat loss through doors occurs in several ways. If a door is opened and closed frequently, heat loss can be considerable. However, passive heat loss can be a problem, too. Passive heat loss occurs when heat seeps out through cracks and gaps around a doorframe. Heat can also escape through the door itself if it is not well insulated.

A doorframe may need **weather stripping** all around it in order to prevent heat loss. Weather stripping consists of pieces of felt, foam rubber, or other bulky material used to seal cracks. Adding a sweep to the bottom of the door also reduces heat loss. A sweep is a flexible piece of rubber or plastic attached to the bottom of the interior side of the door. It drags along the floor as the door opens or closes, blocking the space between the door and the floor.

Airlocks

In climates with cold winters, an airlock behind an exterior door can reduce the amount of heat lost. The revolving doors in many

Airlocks, such as revolving doors, reduce exchange of air with the outside.

commercial buildings are an example of airlocks. In homes, builders may construct a tiny room just inside the main door, with another door closing off the rest of the home's interior. Both of these measures use small buffers of air to limit the interior's exposure to cold, outside air.

The right material

In the past, most doors were made out of wood, but today, doors are constructed from many different materials. Many people prefer the natural, traditional look of wood. However, dense, fine hardwoods are expensive today, and their use can contribute to **deforestation.** One alternative is to find a hardwood door **reclaimed** from a demolished building.

An important consideration is the quality of **insulation** the door provides. Insulation prevents heat from moving from one place to another. Solid wood is a superb insulator. However, if a door has not been properly maintained, it can warp (bend) so that it does not fit well into its frame, causing significant heat loss.

Composite and **vinyl** doors provide good insulation and are sturdy. A composite door is made of materials mixed together for maximum strength and insulation. One type of composite door uses a metal skin with a plastic-foam core. Another type uses **fiberglass** and wood. Fiberglass is a plastic material embedded with thin glass fibers for strength.

Fiberglass and vinyl are both tough materials with excellent insulating qualities. However, they both have high **embodied energy** and require toxic materials to manufacture. Vinyl may give off toxic gases.

energy ☆
ENERGY STAR

Windows

Section Summary

Windows are often the source of heat exchange in a building. Heat enters through windows in summer and escapes through them in winter. Then more energy is needed to keep the building at a comfortable temperature.

Green builders determine where windows should be placed to help make the building energy efficient. They also choose windows that are designed to be energy efficient.

Green architects carefully consider window placement, which can greatly affect lighting and energy use.

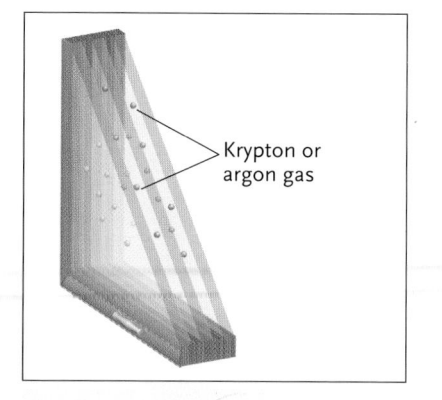

Krypton or argon gas

Air spaces filled with krypton or argon gas provide insulation in double- or triple-pane windows.

Ideally, for nearly perfect **insulation** and energy efficiency, buildings should be windowless. Windows inevitably allow the transfer of some heat between inside and outside. However, the prospect of living and working in environments closed off from the outside world is unacceptable to most people.

Since we value windows, the challenge is to keep heat exchange through and around windows as low as possible. Since the mid-1900's, new and improved technologies have provided ever more options for energy-efficient windows.

Double- and triple-pane windows

Windows with single panes (sheets) of glass provide poor insulation. The glass quickly heats up in summer, or it draws heat away from the building interior in winter. In fact, cold glass panes can make a house feel drafty in cold conditions, even if the window is airtight. As the window chills the interior air in contact with it, that air sinks. The sinking air creates an air current, which feels like a draft.

One solution to this problem is a double-pane window. These windows consist of two glass panes (panels) with space between them for insulation. Often, the space between the panes contains a gas, such as krypton or argon. The gas provides especially good insulation. On a cold day, the outside pane gets as cold as the frigid air, and the inside pane stays as toasty as the heated interior, thanks to the insulating space.

Triple-pane windows consist of three glass panes separated

by insulating spaces. Such windows are especially appropriate for buildings in regions with bitterly cold winters.

Low-e windows

Low-emissivity coating, or "low-e" for short, is another technology that has made windows more energy-efficient. (*Emissivity* comes from the verb *to emit*, which means "to give off.") **Low-e windows** have a special coating of a metal or a metallic compound called metal oxide. The coating largely blocks out strong, direct sunshine but admits weaker, indirect sunshine. Such coatings reflect bright sunshine in summer and admit weaker light in winter, reducing the need for artificial heating and cooling.

Window placement

When architects design buildings, they give considerable thought to where windows should be placed. In the world of green design and construction, the main considerations for window placement are energy efficiency and use of daylight.

In a warm to hot climate in the Northern Hemisphere, it is best to place large windows on the north side of the building, which receives less sunshine. Windows on the hotter, south side of the building should be shaded with overhangs or awnings to reduce heat gain from the sun.

In a cold climate, large windows on the south side provide some wintertime warming from the sun, while more modest windows (and perhaps fewer of them) on the north side minimize heat loss from blasts of northern wind.

The east and west sides of buildings present a greater design challenge. That is because early morning and late afternoon sunshine comes in at low angles. One strategy is to use higher-placed windows on these sides of a building. **Clerestory windows** are often placed in rows high on a wall.

Daylight

Most buildings need some artificial electric light. However, green architects and designers try to make the most of natural daylight to reduce a building's consumption of electricity for lighting. Some of these strategies are considered on pages 26-27.

Clerestory windows can be a green design choice for east and west sides of buildings.

Lighting

Section Summary

Lighting is an important part of a building's design. Green builders find creative ways to make the best use of daylight in buildings. They build constructions that reflect sunlight back into the window without increasing heat. They may also use natural light in combination with energy-efficient light fixtures.

To achieve the most efficient use of energy, green builders incorporate computers and light sensors into lighting systems. The computers control artificial lighting levels based on the amount of daylight available.

Light shelves are designed to reflect light but not heat into the interior of buildings. This building (above) has both interior and exterior light shelves.

Artificial lighting consumes between 20 to 25 percent of the electricity used in the United States. Traditionally, most artificial lighting has been provided by **incandescent light bulbs.** These bulbs do not make efficient use of electricity, however, because they convert a great deal of electricity into heat rather than light. This heat can consume even more electricity by increasing the need for energy-intensive cooling. Green architects and designers seek to reduce this energy use, often through a combination of low-energy electric lights and the use of natural light. (See the "Closer Look" sidebar on page 27 for information on energy-efficient light bulbs.)

During the 1900's, many architects overlooked the most appealing and cost-effective means of lighting buildings: daylight. Of course, daylight cannot provide adequate interior lighting at all times. But it can supplement electric lighting systems and significantly reduce energy consumption. Today, green architects are finding new ways to make the best use of daylight in buildings.

Light shelves and lightpipes

A **light shelf** is a shelf usually placed on the outside lower edge of a window to reflect sunlight back into the window. The light shelf has a surface specially designed to reflect light but not heat. Depending on such factors as the height of the building and sunlight exposure, light shelves can increase the amount of daylight that reaches the interior by 200 percent.

A **lightpipe** is a narrow reflective duct (tube) that channels daylight from a roof surface deeply into a building interior. The bottom of a lightpipe contains a diffuser, which is a panel of semitransparent (partially see-through) material that scatters the incoming light.

Building shape

Green architects design buildings with as much surface area as possible, while rejecting designs that leave much of the building interior inaccessible to

The CCTV headquarters in Beijing, China, makes excellent use of natural light with a striking design.

light. The China Central Television Headquarters in Beijing illustrates how architects can achieve attractive designs while making excellent use of natural light. The building's shape was also designed to withstand strong earthquakes.

Reflective interior surfaces

Another way to maximize daylight inside a building is to use light-colored, reflective surfaces, especially on ceilings and floors. Such interior surfaces can reduce the need for artificial lighting, thus reducing a building's energy use.

Integrated lighting

The greenest designs for interior lighting seamlessly blend daylight and artificial light. To achieve the most efficient use of energy possible, designers incorporate sophisticated computers and light sensors into lighting systems. The computers control artificial lighting levels based on the amount of daylight that is available. Electricity consumption for lighting is low on days with bright sunshine. It is highest at night.

A CLOSER LOOK
Greener Electric Lights

Many consumers are replacing incandescent light bulbs with **compact fluorescent light bulbs (CFL's)**. CFL's are small fluorescent light bulbs that use an electric current to excite electrons in a gas, causing the gas to give off light. CFL's use far less electricity and last far longer than incandescent light bulbs.

Another new low-energy lighting option is the **light-emitting diode, or LED.** LED's require only tiny amounts of electricity, last hundreds of times longer than either incandescent bulbs or CFL's, and produce virtually no heat. However, LED's are currently considerably more expensive than incandescent bulbs. Lighting experts expect these costs to come down over time.

A compact fluorescent light bulb

Roofing

Section Summary

Roofs store much heat from the sun. This increases the amount of energy required to cool the building. Green architects search for ways to reduce heat build-up on roofs.

Some builders cover roofs with materials that help reflect sunlight back into the sky. They may also construct a "green roof" that is covered with plants. Both methods reduce the amount of heat absorbed by the roof. This reduces the amount of energy needed to cool the building.

During the day, roofs can become scorching hot, increasing energy use in buildings.

A roof is like a skin protecting the people and things inside a building from exposure to sunlight and harsh weather. As anyone who has suffered from sunburn knows, sunlight can be quite intense. On a sunny summer day, the temperature on a standard roof can skyrocket to 190 °F (88 °C). The heat build-up significantly increases the building's **cooling load**, or the energy required to cool it. In cities, heat from rooftops contributes to the **heat island effect**, or the concentration of heat in areas densely packed with buildings, roads, and other human-made structures. Green builders search for ways to reduce heat build-up on roofs.

Reflective roofs

One way to make buildings more efficient is to use rooftops that are highly reflective. These rooftops reflect much of the sunlight they receive back into the sky and thereby reduce the heat build-up on the roof. Highly reflective roofs are sometimes called **cool roofs.**

Measuring reflectivity

The scientific term for the amount of sunlight that a surface reflects is **solar reflectance.** Some materials, such as some kinds of glass or shiny metal, have high solar reflectance. Other materials, such as dark wood or brick, have low solar reflectance. Roofs in areas with hot summers should have high solar reflectance. However, solar reflectance is only one part of the story. Roofs also need to have a high level of **thermal emittance**—that is, they should give off much of the heat they do absorb from sunshine.

Standard metal roofs have high solar reflectance but low thermal emittance. A better choice would be a cool roof with a smooth, white surface. Such roofs, with high solar reflectance and high thermal emittance, may be as much as 80 °F (44 °C) cooler in midsummer than conventional roofs. This difference could lead to savings of up to 70 percent in summer energy costs. Installing a cool roof is especially important in places with hot climates.

Cool roofs can be in the form of highly reflective tiles or a white liquid coating that is applied to the roof. Builders can also fasten sheets that are made of rubber or plastic materials to increase the reflectivity of existing roofs. Treated metal roofs are an additional option.

To keep a cool roof highly reflective, workers may need to wash the surface from time to time. Dirt and dust build-up reduces reflectivity and lessens the cool roof's effectiveness.

Lightly colored roofing reflects more sunlight and reduces the need for cooling.

Green roofs, such as Chicago, Illinois,' City Hall rooftop, are Earth-friendly and attractive, creating islands of life in cities.

Green roofs

A **green roof** is a roof that is covered with plants. The plants are not in pots or other containers. Instead, they are part of the roof itself.

Creating a green roof requires a builder with specialized skills and knowledge. The base of the roof must be protected with a waterproof membrane (covering). Then a mesh structure must be created to support the soil and plants. Typically, green roofs use hardy (strong) native plants that grow well without **fertilizers** or **pesticides** (chemicals that kill pests). The idea is to get the roof to grow and flourish naturally.

Keeping temperatures even

Green roofs offer benefits far beyond their visual appeal. Plants absorb sunlight and use it in photosynthesis, the series of chemical reactions by which plants make food. Masses of plants also create zones of higher humidity, because plants draw water into their leaves where it **evaporates** into the air. These features of living plants reduce the cost of cooling and heating a single-story house by 20 to 30 percent. With the top of the building significantly cooler, the building requires less energy-intensive cooling of its interior.

By the same token, a green roof keeps the top of a building warmer in winter. The web of living plants is like a warm coat worn by the building. A green roof thus helps reduce energy use during winter, too.

Conserving water

Roofs collect much water from rain or other forms of precipitation. A roof must shed this water if the interior of the building is to be protected from damaging moisture.

On a standard roof, rainwater rushes into gutters and downspouts toward the ground. In cities and towns, such water is collected in sewers (underground drains), where it mixes with garbage and **pollutants**. This water is carried away and essentially wasted. Unlike standard roofs, green roofs hold onto much of their rainwater, keeping it from gushing into sewers. Some of this water seeps slowly into ground gutters, which funnel water into the landscape. Slow—versus rapid—runoff tends to pick up less garbage and fewer pollutants on its journey.

Filtering air

Green roofs improve the air quality. To conduct photosynthesis, plants take in **carbon dioxide** and give off oxygen. This natural filtering process helps reduce the amount of carbon dioxide in the atmosphere.

Saving wildlife

Where there are masses of plant life, animal life is sure to follow. A green roof creates a **habitat** that attracts birds, insects, and other animals. Green roofs help restore the balance of nature in the artificial environment of built-up urban areas.

Workers construct a green roof on top of a building in New York City.

A CLOSER LOOK
California's Bay Checkerspot Butterfly

Massive urban growth in California during the past 100 years has threatened the survival of many species of wildlife. One densely populated region is the San Francisco Bay area, which includes the cities of San Francisco, San Jose, and Oakland, among others. The Bay area is home to the bay checkerspot, a butterfly with a checkered wing pattern. The bay checkerspot was placed on the U.S. list of endangered and threatened species in 1987. In 2001, the U.S. Fish and Wildlife Service designated nearly 24,000 acres (9,712 hectares) around the edge of San Francisco Bay as a protected area for the butterfly.

Today, a number of builders in the Bay area are installing green roofs with plants to attract bay checkerspots. Scientists believe that if enough of the green roofs are created in the urban area, the bay checkerspot species may bounce back.

Electricity

Section Summary

Electricity used by buildings comes from power plants. Many power plants burn coal for energy. The burning of coal and other fossil fuels releases carbon dioxide, a gas that builds up in Earth's atmosphere and traps heat. Power plants also release other pollutants.

Many green buildings use renewable, pollution-free methods to generate electricity. The sun's energy can be captured in devices called solar panels, which are often placed on rooftops. Wind turbines use energy from the wind to generate electricity.

Buildings consume vast amounts of electricity for climate control and lighting.

Our modern way of life depends upon an endless supply of electric power. Powering everything from laptop computers to huge office towers and factories seems to involve nothing more than "plugging in" to the electrical grid. The ease of using electricity creates the illusion that electricity is clean and inexhaustible.

In reality, our supply of electricity is neither clean nor endless. Electricity comes from power plants, which run huge generators, machines that change mechanical energy into electrical energy. In most cases, power plants run the generators by burning such a **fossil fuel** as coal, oil, or natural gas. Heat from the burning fuel is used to spin **turbines** (wheellike objects), which creates an electrical current in wire circuits.

Much of the electricity used in the world today is generated by burning coal, a highly polluting fossil fuel. Gases given off by coal-burning power plants contribute significantly to **carbon dioxide** build-up in Earth's **atmosphere**. Burning coal can also release other **pollutants** that are harmful to people and wildlife.

Almost all consumers of electricity are "connected to the grid." The **power grid** is the interconnected system of power plants, transmission wires, and consumers of electricity. To keep the grid "hot" with electricity, at least some power plants must be running at all times, because electricity is difficult to store. Buildings that generate their own electricity can contribute some electricity back to the grid. If enough buildings and homeowners go green, it will eventually be possible to cut back on burning fossil fuels in power plants.

Energy alternatives

Today, architects and individuals are seeking ways to generate electricity within buildings in order to reduce the amount of electricity needed from public power plants. Two attractive methods of generating electricity locally are **solar power** and wind power.

Solar power

Think about all the energy in the sunlight that streams down on a bright, sunny day. If we could harvest enough of that energy, fossil fuels would no longer be needed. However, capturing the energy in sunlight is not easy.

Today, we do have a technology that directly converts sunlight into electricity. It is called solar power. Solar power is created by a device similar to the tiny transistors in computers. This device is called a **solar cell.** One solar cell exposed to direct sunlight produces a tiny electrical current—far less than is needed to light a single light bulb. To generate a useful amount of electricity, many cells are combined in **solar panels.** A solar panel is a flat, thin panel of solar cells with a large surface area to collect as much sunlight as possible.

Solar panels cannot do the heavy-duty work of giant generators in coal-burning power plants, but they can make an important contribution to the energy supply. The panels are easy to incorporate into building designs by placing them on roofs. Panels can also be placed on separate mounts in open areas. Some panels are designed to tilt automatically to follow the sun's movement. However, it is important to place the panels so that shadows, such as from tree branches or utility poles, do not fall on the solar cells.

The government of Australia recently funded the development of "solar shades" for school campuses. The structures provide shade for students and also collect solar energy.

Dedicated solar power in buildings

In larger, more complex buildings, architects often allocate electricity generated by solar panels to specific jobs. Such specific uses of power are called dedicated solar power. For example, some green office buildings have automated shading systems on western-facing windows to reduce heat gain during the sunny afternoon hours. Such systems often consist of special slats that can open and shut. A solar panel can easily supply the power needed to move the slats. Solar panels can also provide power for the fans in a building's **ventilation** system.

When the sun doesn't shine

Dark, overcast days—as well as nighttime—pose obvious problems for generating solar power. Since the need for electricity is constant, solar power does have a major downside. One solution to this problem is using solar panels that are connected to rechargeable batteries. Battery power has its limits, however. In extended periods of overcast days, the battery backup might run out, too. For this reason, solar power is often used in combination with another power source, such as wind power.

Wind power

For thousands of years, people have harnessed wind as a power source. The wind **turbines** we use today are sleek and high-tech. Turbines use wind energy to turn curved blades that are attached to a moving axel. The movement of the axel causes the generator to turn, which changes the wind energy into electricity. Wind turbine generators are typically connected to the electrical grid.

Wind turbines and large buildings

Some of the world's greenest buildings are designed with both solar panels and wind turbines. Typically, designers place the wind turbines in the upper parts of tall buildings to take advantage of stronger winds aloft.

Home wind turbines

Homeowners can install a wind turbine to add to their electricity supply. Typically, homeowners arrange for a tie-in to the grid and receive reductions in their electric bills in exchange for the wind-generated electricity they contribute. A home turbine is expensive, usually costing between $10,000 and $50,000 or more. Over time, however, homeowners can recover these costs through savings in electricity bills.

To be effective, the turbine must be mounted on a shaft that is at least 80 feet (24 meters) tall. That is because wind speeds are typically higher at that altitude (height) and there is less turbulence (interruptions in wind flow) caused by objects at ground level. Installing a high tower in a rural area is usually not a problem, but cities and suburbs are another matter. Many towns and cities have laws that restrict heights of built structures. Such laws might prevent some homeowners and small businesses from installing wind turbine towers.

Wind power is not constant, and it is most effective in areas that are frequently windy. Like solar power, it must be supported by other power sources.

Some electric power companies get part of their power supply from wind turbines.

Water Use

Section Summary

Water use in some countries exceeds what water sources can support. Today, experts are warning of approaching water shortages in many parts of the world.

Green architects incorporate ways to save and reuse water into their buildings' design. These methods include reusing water that drains from kitchen sinks and showers or collecting rainwater. The collected water can be used for landscape watering, or it can be lightly filtered for flushing toilets and other uses.

Many areas have begun to suffer water shortages, as people use ever more water.

Today, water experts are warning of approaching water shortages in many parts of the world. They point to such signs as retreating glaciers and shrinking freshwater lakes and reservoirs around the world. In January 2008, Secretary-General of the **United Nations** Ban Ki-moon warned of global water shortages and urged governments and corporations to take action.

The "magic" water tap

For many people, daily life involves almost constant use of water. We can turn on water taps at any time—and out flows clean, fresh water. What's left of our used water goes down the drain, and we rarely think of what happens next.

In reality, the water we use is part of a continuous loop. The clean water on which we depend has been treated at a water treatment plant to make it safe to drink. Our used water travels through pipes to a **sewage** treatment plant. The treated water is released into rivers or lakes, where some of it is drawn into a water treatment plant—and so continues the loop. Treating water requires energy, most of which comes from **fossil-fuel**-burning power plants.

Landscaping

The landscape surrounding buildings can be a source of much water use. For example, grass may be planted in dry climates and require constant watering. Landscape irrigation in the United States accounts for almost one-third of all residential water use, equaling more than 7 billion gallons (26.5 billion liters) per day.

Conserving water

In the past, many buildings were built with water tanks to collect rainwater from draining roofs. Although such water could not be safely drunk unless specially treated, it could be used for such purposes as washing clothes or watering landscape plants. Gradually, builders stopped providing water tanks because most people believed that supplies of clean, fresh water would never run out. Today, however, we know that fresh water is one of Earth's most precious resources. As a result, green-thinking builders today are finding ways—old and new—to save and reuse water.

Water basics

Water that has been used in homes, offices, and schools is generally described as wastewater. However, there are two types of wastewater. Water that flushes from toilets is called **blackwater.** This water must be treated thoroughly in a sewage treatment plant before it can be reused or flushed into rivers and streams. Water that drains from kitchen sinks and showers, along with rainwater, is called **graywater.** Graywater can be reused in some ways without having to go back through a sewage treatment plant. For example, it can be used to flush toilets or to water landscapes.

Traditionally, both blackwater and graywater from buildings are treated at a sewage treatment plant.

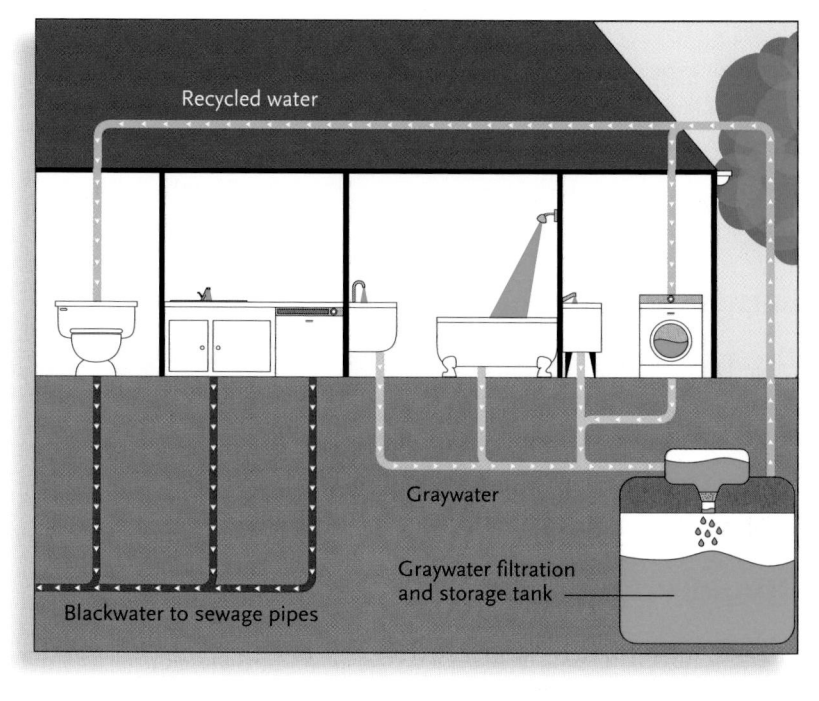

Some buildings have a storage tank for graywater. The water can then be used to water the landscape or for some indoor uses.

Labels in diagram: Recycled water · Graywater · Graywater filtration and storage tank · Blackwater to sewage pipes

The reeds and other plants in artificial wetlands naturally filter and cleanse graywater.

Recycling graywater

Recycling graywater is an excellent way to cut water use and water waste. Some of the world's most imaginative architects have relied on nature's own patterns to develop ways to filter graywater for uses other than drinking water.

Graywater can be strained through a layer of sand, which acts like a natural filter. Then, the water can be channeled into an artificial wetland created as part of the building's design. The wetland includes plant life, such as reeds. The reeds and other plant life naturally filter and cleanse the water as it drains through the wetland. Water collected at the lower end of the wetland is then clean enough for flushing toilets and other **nonpotable** uses.

The miracle of rain

About 900 years ago, the Anasazi (*AH nuh SAH zee*) people of present-day Colorado and New Mexico devised clever ways to trap scarce rainwater to grow their crops in a dry climate. People today are renewing their interest in catching and saving rainwater, and leading architects are designing systems in buildings to save rainwater.

One of the best places to collect rainfall is on a building's roof. The roof surface area of an average-size house can collect a surprisingly large volume of water. This water can be collected in gutters along the roof eaves (overhangs) and channeled into downspouts leading to tanks. The collected water can be used for landscape watering, or it can be lightly filtered for flushing toilets or washing clothes.

Just good common sense

Some water-saving features are so simple that they can easily be added to any building design or rehab project. (*Rehab* is from *rehabilitation,* meaning "to fix up.") Taken together, the items listed below can greatly reduce a building's water use.

- More efficient faucets: High-tech faucets that carefully control water flow save a surprising amount of water.
- Aerating showerheads: By introducing air bubbles into the water stream, these showerheads create desirable pressure levels with less water flow than standard showerheads.
- Dual-flush toilets: These toilets allow the user to choose a higher- or lower-volume flush, saving water when possible.
- Waterless urinals: Urinals made of materials that self-clean, so that water does not have to be flushed, save much water in a high-volume office or public bathroom.

Rain barrels collect rainwater and save it for watering gardens and other uses.

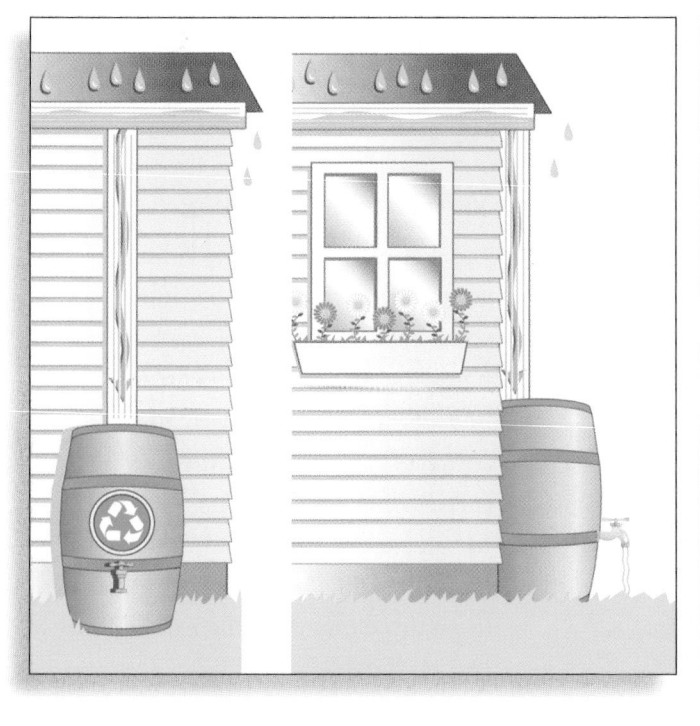

Heating and Cooling

Section Summary

Heating and cooling buildings requires much energy. Some architects have designed ways to reduce the need for artificial climate control. For example, they use floors made of materials that absorb heat during the day and release it at night. They create "chimneys" that release rising, warm air from the building. Some techniques are much simpler, such as using window shades during sunny parts of the day.

Warm-air heating systems (below) may be supplemented with such heating devices as wood-burning stoves (above).

To provide healthy, pleasant environments for living and working, buildings must be cooled in hot weather and heated in cold weather. Most heating and cooling methods require much energy to work.

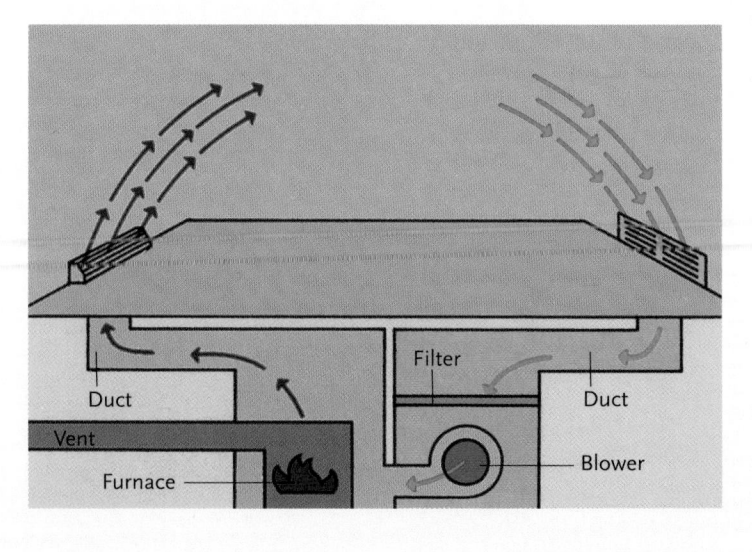

Duct

Vent

Furnace

Filter

Duct

Blower

Warm-air heating

Today, much of our indoor heat comes from furnaces that burn some type of **fossil fuel**, such as natural gas or heating oil from **petroleum**. In houses with such furnaces, an opening called a vent carries exhaust (spent gases) from the furnace to the outside air. This exhaust contains many **pollutants**, but the main element of the exhaust is **carbon dioxide**.

Mechanical refrigeration

Cooling a building often involves **mechanical refrigeration**. Mechanical refrigeration relies on two basic scientific principles of heat exchange: A liquid absorbs heat when it changes into a gas (the process of **evaporation**); and a gas gives up heat when it changes back into a liquid (the process of **condensation**).

In mechanical refrigeration, a liquid called a **refrigerant** enters the system's evaporator, where it changes into a gas, absorbing heat from the surrounding area. Later in the cycle, a device called a compressor squeezes the gas. The gas is then changed back into a liquid in the system's condenser, giving up heat, which is typically channeled to the outside of the building. Thus, heat is continually drawn away from air inside the building and discarded outside.

Continually squeezing gas inside a compressor requires considerable energy. This explains why people's electric bills shoot up during hot weather, when air conditioners must be used continually to maintain cool temperatures inside the building.

Green strategies

Buildings designed for natural cooling require much less mechanical refrigeration than other buildings. By the same token, buildings designed for efficient heating minimize fuel consumption and save energy. Reducing the need for heating and cooling inside buildings is the first step toward greener climate control. The following pages describe some of the current strategies for reducing energy consumption from heating and cooling buildings.

Solar heating is a green strategy that uses heat energy from the sun to keep homes warm in winter. In summer, overhangs shade the windows to keep rooms from absorbing heat.

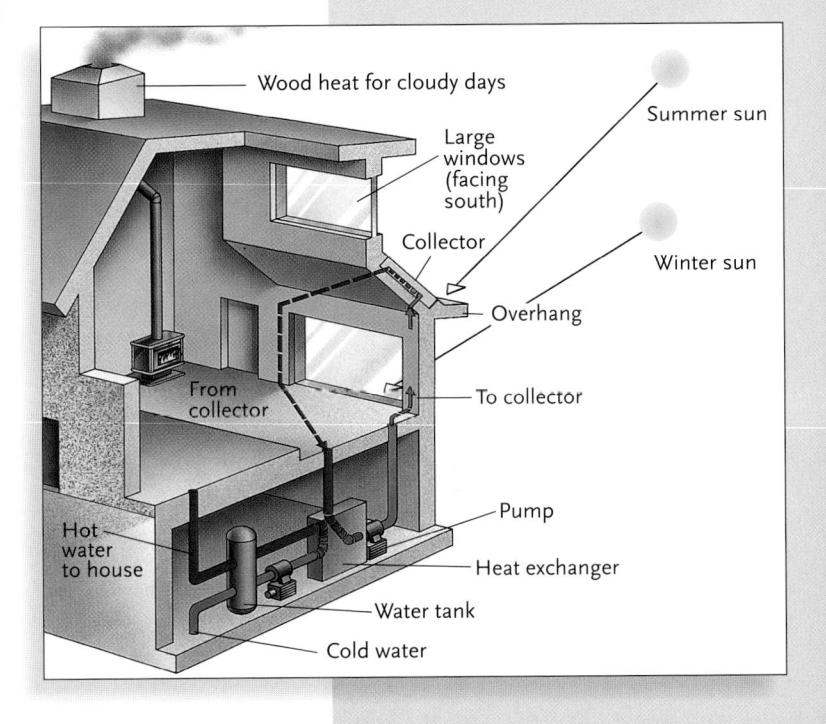

Wood heat for cloudy days

Large windows (facing south)

Collector

Overhang

From collector

To collector

Summer sun

Winter sun

Pump

Heat exchanger

Hot water to house

Water tank

Cold water

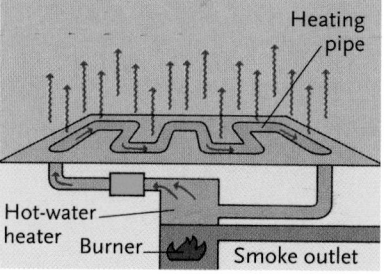

Many radiant heating systems include pipes underneath the floor that circulate heated water.

Radiant heating and cooling

Most heating and cooling systems work by heating or cooling air and then venting it through buildings, which is both inefficient and energy-intensive. However, **radiant heating and cooling** systems rely on a different principle. Instead of heating or cooling air, a radiant system heats or cools an object, such as a floor. Heat always moves from warmer to cooler areas, so the heat from a radiant floor moves into objects in contact with the floor, making them warmer. By the same principle, a cool floor attracts heat from objects in the room. That withdrawal of heat cools the objects, thus removing heat from the room.

Radiant heating and cooling work best with structures that have high **thermal mass**. For example, thick stone or concrete floors retain heat or cold for a long time and change temperature slowly.

Typically, a radiant climate control system includes a network of water pipes built into the floor or some other structure with high thermal mass. In winter, warm water flowing through the pipes provides heat that radiates from the floor. In summer, cool water draws away heat from the floor, which in turn draws away heat from the room above it.

Thermal chimneys

Long before modern air conditioning was invented, people learned how to cool down hot buildings by drawing in cooler air from outside sources and venting warm air from inside the building. This process of exchanging inside air for outside air is called **ventilation**. Today, green designers and builders are drawing on ventilation techniques to reduce the need for energy-intensive cooling inside buildings.

One device that helps establish a cycle of airflow through a building is the **thermal chimney**. A thermal chimney is a hollow tower through which rising, warm air escapes the building. This natural upward movement of heated air into and through the thermal chimney creates an air current that draws in cooler air at lower levels. A thermal tower through which rising, warm air escapes the building. This natural upward movement of heated air into and through the thermal chimney creates an air current that draws in cooler air at lower

Cool towers, such as this one (left) at the Zion National Park Visitor Center in Utah, use evaporation to cool air drawn into the building.

levels. A thermal chimney design is best combined with ventilating windows lower in the building.

Shower towers and cool towers

Some green cooling systems make use of shower towers. Shower towers are enclosed towers in which fine water droplets are showered down. As the droplets fall through the air, some of the water is evaporated. Because the process of evaporating water absorbs heat, the air and the water at the bottom of the tower are cooler than at the top. The cool air and water can be used in a variety of ways to cool building interiors. For example, the cool water can be directed through pipe systems for radiant cooling. The cool air can be vented into warm rooms. Because shower towers rely on evaporation, they work best in dry climates.

Cool towers use similar cooling techniques. Cool towers often include pads at the top of the tower, which are sprayed with water. As the water evaporates, it removes heat from the air. The cool, dense air then moves down the tower and circulates inside the building.

Shower towers cool the air by evaporating water droplets as they fall.

Cold outside air temperatures

Room air returns to handler

Warmed air is distributed through the house

Air handler

Relatively warm ground

Underground pipes

Compressor

Heat is transfered to air inside the air handler

Cold liquid flows through coils, absorbing heat from warmer water in ground loop

Some geothermal heating systems circulate a fluid through underground pipes, which carry the heat of the ground into the building.

Desiccant systems

A **desiccant** is a substance that attracts water and is thus capable of drawing water vapor out of humid air. In climates with humid summers, high humidity can make people feel uncomfortable even when the temperature itself is moderate. Thus, one way to reduce conventional, high-energy air conditioning is simply to remove the humidity from air.

A desiccant cooling system includes a rotating wheel over which incoming air blows. The wheel is filled with desiccants. As the air flows over the wheel, the desiccants absorb the moisture, so that relatively dry air fills the building interior. For the desiccants to continue doing their job, energy is required to remove moisture from the desiccants themselves. This energy requirement is less than the energy that would be required to run a conventional air conditioning system.

Geothermal heating and cooling

Unlike Earth's surface, the ground 5 to 10 feet (1.5 to 3 meters) below the surface remains at nearly constant temperatures, typically in the range of 50 to 60 °F (10 to 16 °C). Wells drilled in the ground usually fill up with water in this temperature range. In cold weather, **geothermal** heating systems extract heat from this relatively warm water to heat buildings. In hot weather, geothermal systems can circulate the relatively cool well water through pipes to cool buildings. Alternatively, a geothermal system may consist of an interconnected network of in-building and underground pipes filled with a nontoxic liquid operating upon similar principles.

Light shading

One very effective strategy for reducing heat build-up in buildings is to use window coverings to reflect warming sunlight.

This cooling strategy can be as simple as pulling down shades in the afternoon on the west wall of a building. Some buildings have automated shading systems that shut out sunlight during hot weather and admit sunlight at other times.

Automated light-shading systems that block sunlight during the brightest part of the day can help reduce energy costs.

Integrated design

Green architects, engineers, and designers are finding that the greenest solutions to heating and cooling challenges often combine many technologies in sophisticated ways. For example, thermal chimneys might be alternated with a certain amount of mechanical refrigeration to achieve comfort in an energy-efficient way. Such techniques as light shading or evaporative cooling might be used to keep a building from heating up in the first place. Computers and electric sensors can be used to continually adjust window shades, increasing efficiency.

A CLOSER LOOK
"Cool" Lessons from Termites

Some architects have looked to nature to develop cooling strategies for buildings. Termites in Africa build dried-mud mounds that contain thousands of honeycombed air passages and are built tall to catch breezes. The mud structure has a high thermal mass, helping temperatures stay cool inside.

The Eastgate building in Harare, Zimbabwe, uses a ventilation system similar to the termite mounds. Air is brought into the building and heated or cooled by the building's mass. It is then vented through the building before escaping through chimneys.

Landscaping

Section Summary

Landscaping involves shaping the land and vegetation around a building. Green architects carefully consider ways to use landscaping to make buildings more efficient. For example, they position buildings on the land in a way that fits with its natural surroundings. They conserve water and use natural gardening practices rather than artificial or chemical methods. They also choose plants that are native to an area and require little maintenance.

Architects of the Jubilee Campus of the University of Nottingham made the campus's lake an essential part of their design.

Landscaping includes all actions involved in improving or preserving a plot of land for human use and appreciation. In green architecture, landscaping also involves working with nature—instead of against it—in positioning buildings on the land. It also means conserving water and using natural gardening practices rather than artificial or chemical methods.

Why landscaping is important

For a truly green building, landscaping is an inseparable part of the building's design. The quality of the landscape has a big impact on **ventilation** and temperature control, for example. Picture a strip mall in an urban area. If the shops are surrounded by nothing but large areas of pavement, the whole plot of land absorbs sunlight and radiates heat like an enormous skillet. On the other hand, if the strip mall has been developed with plenty of plantings and trees to interrupt large spans of pavement, the strip mall's temperatures will stay cooler, even on hot, sunny days.

A landscape-integrated green campus

The Jubilee Campus of the University of Nottingham contains some of the greenest architecture in the United Kingdom. The campus was designed by the London-based architecture firm Michael Hopkins and Partners and opened in 1999. The buildings are highly integrated into the landscape, which is used to contribute to cooling and water conservation. The campus is oriented around a lakeside arcade (covered passageway). Winds from the lake naturally cool the arcade and various building **atriums**.

Green principles of landscaping

The Jubilee Campus illustrates one principle of green landscaping: integrating buildings into the landscape. Other important principles include:

- Conserving water and enhancing, rather than replacing, natural drainage.
- Using nature as much as possible to minimize human intervention and maintenance.
- Eliminating strong chemical **fertilizers** and **pesticides**.
- Maximizing airflow and natural cooling strategies.

All of these principles can be summarized in one guideline: Keep it natural!

Using water wisely

Experts estimate that more than 15 percent of household water is used to water landscape plants. In an era of growing water scarcity, this is a practice that cannot be sustained.

A number of strategies for water conservation in landscapes are available. One of the greenest approaches is capturing rainwater in a water tank for use in landscape watering. Tying the system into rainwater runoff from a building's rooftop is the most effective way to gather water. Using rainwater for landscape watering reduces demand on public water systems.

A CLOSER LOOK
Xeriscape Gardening

In such water-challenged areas as the southwestern United States, xeriscape (*ZIHR uh skayp*) gardening has caught on with many landscape designers and homeowners. The term *xeriscape* comes from the Greek root *xeros*, meaning "dry," plus "landscape."

Xeriscaping is a strategy for gardening that emphasizes methods that conserve water, and it calls for the use of drought-tolerant plants, such as cactuses. Often, xeriscape landscapes use visually attractive rocks, sand, or other nonliving materials to fill spaces between plantings, rather than water-hungry grass.

Xeriscape gardening

Grass paving uses pavers with holes, allowing water to drain and grass to grow.

Drainage in the landscape

In a natural landscape, much of the rainwater percolates down into the soil and eventually becomes part of ground water (water held beneath the earth's surface), while excess rainwater runs off into rivers and streams. Because so much of the environment in urban areas is built up, natural drainage is often disrupted.

One way to encourage natural drainage is to limit paved areas and to use **permeable paving**—paving that allows rainwater to drain through it. Porous types of asphalt and concrete are available for permeable paving, but these materials have high **embodied energy.** Stone or brick paving may require less energy to produce while still allowing plenty of natural drainage. Other green alternatives include gravel, river rock, and grass paving. Grass paving involves using pavement with holes in which grass can be planted. The finished effect is a checkerboard of paving material and grass patches.

Permeable paving provides many benefits. It reduces rapid runoff, or the gushing volumes of water that can wash a variety of **pollutants** into storm sewers. It also reduces the risk of storm flooding.

Another strategy to improve drainage is the use of **rain gardens**. A rain garden is a shallow depression in a landscape in which native, deep-rooted plants are grown. The function of a rain garden is to allow rainwater to collect and drain slowly into the soil. Rain gardens reduce runoff into sewer systems and filter pollutants from water that will eventually pass into ground water.

The costs of green lawns

To many people, a landscape isn't complete without large expanses of manicured, emerald-green grass. However, we may not be able to afford our love of grassy lawns. Such lawns are planted in varieties of turf grass. Most turf grasses require heavy watering, along with heavy use of fertilizers and pesticides, if they are to remain "perfect." The intensive use of water depletes water supplies, and toxic chemical fertilizers and pesticides wash into streams and ground water.

A greener approach to lawns is to alternate small areas of turf grass with native plantings. Also, landscapers may use more drought-tolerant varieties of turf grass. Managing lawns sensibly and **sustainably** may also require living with browned-out grass during dry seasons. Often, such grass has moved water down into its roots to survive the dry weather. It will quickly become green again when rain returns.

In the long run, landscapes are healthiest and easiest to maintain when planted with native grasses, flowers, and shrubs. The appropriate varieties of plant material vary from one geographic region to another. A botanical garden or arboretum (a garden that specializes in tree cultivation) is a good resource for finding out which plants are native to your area.

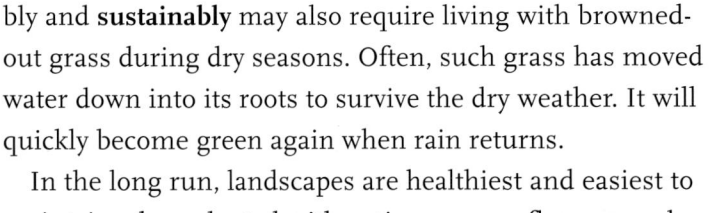

Such water-intensive landscapes as golf courses can strain water supplies in regions with dry climates.

The benefits of trees

Trees provide many benefits to the environment. Trees have extensive, deep roots that hold the soil and prevent erosion. Like other living plants, they absorb **carbon dioxide** and give off oxygen. Trees also provide a **habitat** for much wildlife, including squirrels, insects, and many species of birds.

On hot summer days, many people seek shelter underneath the shade of trees. Similarly, green architects and landscapers use trees to keep buildings cool, improving the building's energy efficiency. In urban landscapes, trees play an especially important role in climate control by shading buildings and reducing summertime heat gain.

Trees offer many benefits, including providing shade that reduces the need for cooling.

Green Buildings

Section Summary

Green buildings are becoming more common around the world. The Council House 2 building, in Melbourne, Australia, has drawn attention for its environmentally-friendly and attractive design. Sidwell Friends Middle School, in Washington, D.C., demonstrates how older buildings can be renovated to increase energy efficiency.

Individuals have created unique "extreme green" buildings. These are often made from environmentally-friendly materials, such as mud, straw, or recycled tires.

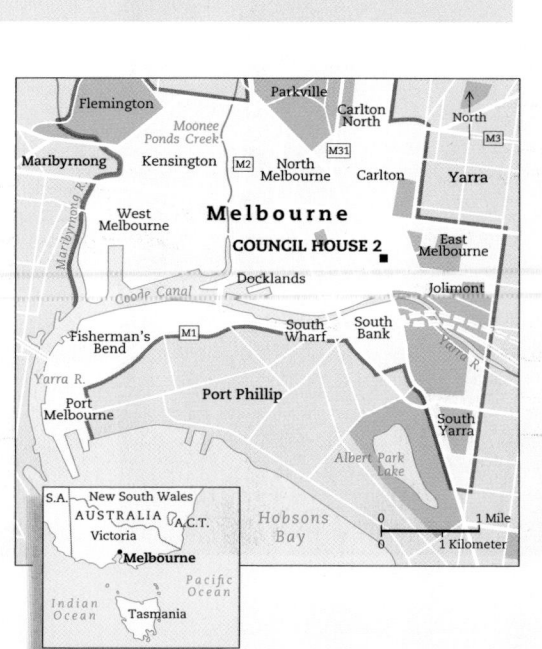

Council House 2 in Melbourne, Australia, is a showcase of green building design.

MELBOURNE'S COUNCIL HOUSE 2

Melbourne, Australia's second-largest city, is becoming a center for green architecture. The city's 10-story Council House 2 (CH2) in downtown Melbourne is one of the greenest buildings in the world today. The building is an office center mainly for the City of Melbourne.

Integrated green systems

Designed by architects from Melbourne-based DesignInc in close collaboration with city officials, Melbourne's Council House 2 is intended to resemble natural Earth ecologies. In nature, organisms and the environment interact in thousands of ways in a seamless web. In a similar way, the various systems in CH2—such as cooling, heating, lighting, and energy generation—are seamlessly integrated. The goal of this green design is to provide an Earth-friendly and healthy working environment.

Council House 2 opened in August 2006. It has won many environmental and architectural awards, including six Green Stars, the highest rating given by the Green Building Council of Australia. Other awards include those from the **United Nations** and the Royal Australian Institute of Architects.

Ventilation

CH2 is designed to circulate fresh air through the entire building. Studies show that building interiors often contain higher levels of **pollutants** than outside air. Furthermore, some **synthetic materials**, such as many plastics, slowly give off toxic gases.

At the heart of CH2's **ventilation** system is a row of six bright yellow wind **turbines** on the building's summit. These turbines are not used to generate electricity. Rather, they draw fresh air from the rooftop level down into the building.

Heating and cooling

The designers of CH2 incorporated a variety of cooling strategies into the structure. Five shower towers cool air and water by **evaporation.** The cooled water is channeled through pipes in thick concrete ceilings with high **thermal mass** to provide **radiant cooling**, while the cool air is vented into warm rooms. Also, the automated shading system, which gives CH2's west front such a distinctive woody look, reduces the building's need for cooling.

A gas-fired generator in the building provides heating. Gas-fired generators produce electricity but waste much heat. In CH2, almost all the heat that would ordinarily be wasted is captured and used to heat water that provides **radiant heating**.

Water use

CH2 has an on-site water treatment plant that draws water from city sewers and cleanses it for use as **graywater** in the building. The building also has rainwater storage tanks, which provide additional graywater. CH2 uses approximately half as much water from city water supplies as a traditional building of the same size.

Electricity

Solar panels on the roof contribute to the building's electrical needs. A gas-fired generator supplements the **solar power**. CH2 was designed to reduce electricity consumption by 85 percent compared with a traditional building.

Bright yellow turbines on top of CH2 draw in fresh air and send it through the building.

SIDWELL FRIENDS MIDDLE SCHOOL

Schools are going green, too. Schools are prime candidates for green design. They are numerous, and most are large buildings housing hundreds of students. The U.S. Green Building Council, the American Federation of Teachers, and other national organizations sponsored a report entitled "Greening America's Schools: Costs and Benefits," which was published in October 2006. The report emphasized that the health and learning of school children could be significantly improved by building and refurbishing America's schools using green technologies.

One of the greenest schools in the world today is the Middle School of the Sidwell Friends School, a private Quaker school in Washington, D.C. The school opened in 2001 as a renovation of a building constructed in 1950. By renovating, rather than building from scratch, the school trustees substantially reduced the energy consumed by the project.

The Sidwell Friends Middle School is built with many recycled materials.

Recycling fervor

Sidwell Friends Middle School is a showcase of recycled materials. The building exterior is covered in western red cedar recovered from old wine casks. Window trim is fashioned from old, dismantled bleachers. Wood from an old pier in Baltimore, Maryland, is also used in the building.

The building's interior features rugs woven from recycled fibers and ceiling tiles fashioned from recycled newspapers. Elsewhere, the building incorporates materials from rapidly **renewable resources.** Doors and floors are made from bamboo. Cabinets are made from wheatboard, a product made by pressing together wheat stalks.

Water recycling

The Sidwell Friends School is a national leader in using constructed wetlands as a filter for graywater. The school campus in-

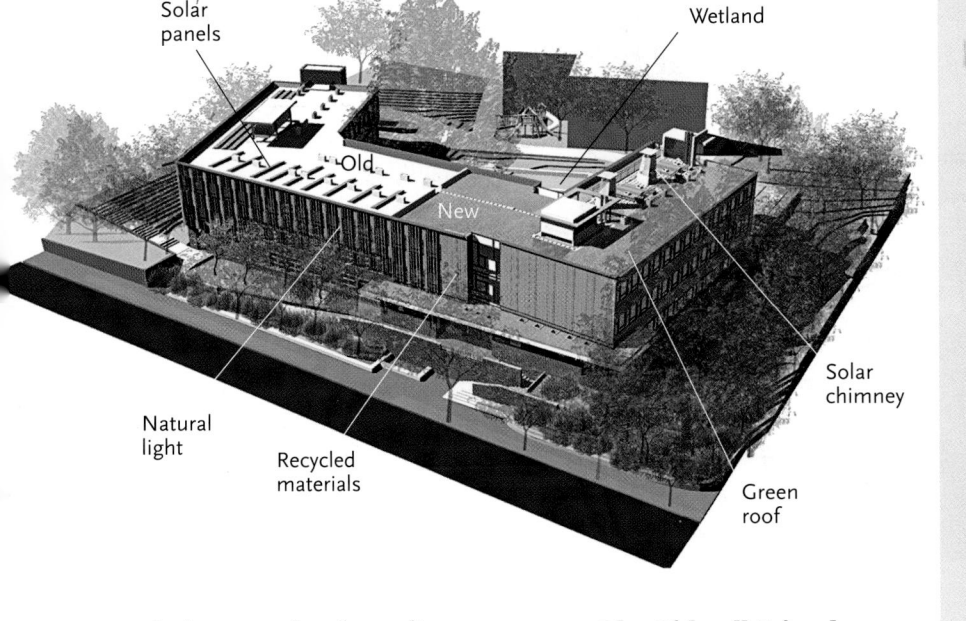

Solar panels

Wetland

Old

New

Natural light

Recycled materials

Solar chimney

Green roof

cludes a pond and an adjacent terraced wetlands area. Graywater from the school is pumped underground into a tank for first-stage treatment. It then percolates through the soil of the wetland, where water plants finish the filtering job. The clean water is returned to the school building for use in toilets and cooling machinery. The school uses about 90 percent less water than a traditional school building of the same size.

The Sidwell Friends Middle School building displays many green architectural principles.

Temperature control and lighting

Like other green buildings, the Sidwell Friends Middle School uses many passive techniques to keep the structure relatively cool in summer and relatively warm in winter. These effects greatly reduce the need for energy-intensive cooling and heating. Features for controlling temperature extremes include **thermal chimneys** with hot zones at the top. These chimneys set up ventilation that pulls cooler air in through low, north-facing windows and releases hot air from the chimney tops. Another temperature-**regulating** feature is the school's insulating **green roof.**

Lighting in the school makes the most of available daylight, with skylights, reflective interior coatings, and light shelves. Computer-controlled electric lights dim or brighten in response to natural conditions.

For those who want to go all the way green, there are less conventional building options, such as cob houses, straw bale houses, earthships, earthbags, and rammed earth buildings. Such structures may seem primitive to some people, but to others, they are forward-thinking and visionary. The following pages describe some of the more "extreme" green building techniques used today.

Staw bale has low embodied energy and provides excellent insulation.

This image shows an early stage in the construction of a straw bale house.

Cob house

Cob is an ancient building material made from clay, sand, and straw fibers. (It has nothing to do with corncobs.) People build cob structures by taking "gobs" of the mixed-up material by hand and piling it up. Cob houses often look like freeform sculpture.

Straw bale house

Typically, builders construct a straw bale house by filling spaces in a frame with straw bales. Both sides are then covered with plaster or adobe. The bales are highly insulating, so straw bale houses tend to be energy efficient. However, if the plaster seal is faulty, moisture or insects can get into the straw and ruin it.

Earthship

An earthship is a structure made by stacking old tires filled with earth to create walls. The interior tire wall is usually plastered over. Earthships have great green appeal because they recycle junked tires, which can be very harmful to the environment if they are improperly discarded.

Earthbag

An earthbag is a structure created by stacking filled sandbags and covering both sides with plaster. The bags can be filled with dry sand, soil, or gravel.

Rammed earth

The rammed earth technique creates walls by tamping (pressing tightly together) soil within forms. This is the building method that was used to construct parts of the Great Wall of China. Rammed earth construction creates very thick walls of 12 inches (30 centimeters) or more, so its **insulation** properties are excellent. Interior walls are typically finished with a natural oil or other sealant.

Going off the grid

For some people, going green means generating 100 percent of their household electricity. When this goal is achieved, it is no longer necessary to be attached to the national electrical grid. However, "going off the grid" doesn't mean that people have to retreat to a premodern lifestyle. A self-sufficient home electrical system can include solar power, wind power, battery backup, and a fuel-driven generator for use when all else fails.

To some people, the idea of going off the grid is a bit scary. If the home system crashes, modern life comes to a halt. Going off the grid requires dedication and a certain amount of daring. Fortunately, there are many ways to be green and remain connected.

Earthship buildings recycle old tires, using them to build walls filled with earth.

Government Action

Section Summary

Government action to support the construction of more energy-efficient buildings has included establishing laws to promote green building techniques. Building codes, which are standards that architects must follow, are becoming greener.

The U.S. federal government and many state governments are also encouraging homeowners to go green. They give tax credits to homeowners who choose to adopt certain green practices, such as solar or wind power.

Many governments have begun to adopt green building codes.

The green architecture movement is taking place against a backdrop of increasing concern about the environment and **global warming**. All around the world, governments are considering what their response should be.

Building codes

Many governments, especially those at the local level, pass building codes that detail how structures should be built. Building codes around the world are becoming greener. Some building codes, for example, require that energy-efficient heating and cooling systems be installed.

In the United States, many cities have adopted green building codes. A code adopted by the city of Chicago sets minimum requirements for the **solar reflectance** of new or replaced roofs on commercial buildings. The goal of these rules is to reduce the **heat island effect** in urban areas.

California has led the way in promoting green architecture in the United States. In 2008, the city government of San Francisco passed a law that sets standards for conserving energy and water for all new construction. That same year, California became the first state to adopt a statewide green building code, which will reduce energy and water consumption by all buildings.

Tax credits

The U.S. federal government and many state governments give tax credits to homeowners who choose to adopt certain green practices. For example, the Energy Policy Act of 2005 provided for federal tax credits to homeowners who installed energy-efficient furnaces, central air conditioning, and **insulation.** It also offered credits to homeowners who bought energy-efficient appliances, such as refrigerators, dishwashers, and clothes washers. The federal government and various state governments offer tax credits to homeowners who use wind or **solar power.**

Metering systems

Most residential energy suppliers—such as homeowners with their own solar and wind power systems—gain an advantage by returning power to the grid in the form of a credit against their electric bills. To encourage this arrangement, many state governments have passed laws requiring energy companies to set up metering systems that measure electricity coming into the grid as well as that going out to consumers.

The federal energy act

In December 2007, the U.S. Congress passed and President George W. Bush signed into law the Energy Independence and Security Act of 2007. Among other provisions, this act set up a federal office that would establish green energy guidelines for all federal buildings. It also requires that all general purpose lighting in federal buildings use energy-efficient lighting by 2013.

The United States has lagged behind some other countries in adopting green building **regulations.** In Europe, regulatory agencies began setting green building standards in the mid-1990's. As a result, European construction today is among the greenest in the world.

 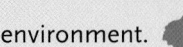
Homeowners' alternative energy sources, such as solar power, may be paid for by returning power to the grid.

Activities

SIMPLE HOME FIXES

Introduction

Green architectural principles can greatly reduce the overall impact of buildings on the environment, but there are many ways we can make existing buildings more environmentally friendly. Try these simple steps to make your home more energy efficient.

In Summer:

- Close curtains on south- and west-facing windows during the day.
- Install white window shades, drapes, or blinds to reflect heat away from the house.
- Install ceiling fans or use window fans to keep rooms cool.

In Winter:

- Keep windows on the south side of your house clean to let in winter sun.
- Close curtains and shades at night to keep heat inside.
- Install a clear plastic film on drafty windows.
- Turn off kitchen, bath, and other ventilating fans within 20 minutes after you are finished cooking or bathing to retain heated air.
- If you use an oven, leave it open after you turn it off to let heat escape into the room.

TEST YOUR HOME FOR AIR LEAKS

Introduction

Homes often have numerous sources of air leaks, which cause more energy to be expended in order to heat or cool our homes. According to the U.S. Department of Energy, reducing air leaks in the home can add up to 5 to 30 percent in energy savings each year. Windows, doors, fireplaces, wood floors with space between the planks, and places where telephone, cable, and gas lines enter the home are common sources of air leaks. Ask an adult to help you test your home for air leaks.

Materials:

- Candle and candleholder
- Matches

Caulking

Directions:

1. Place a candle in a candleholder and ask an adult to light it.
2. On a windy day, hold the lit candle near a window. If the flame of the candle wavers, too much air is leaking in from the outside. You can minimize air leaks through caulking (using a cement-like substance to fill in gaps where air is leaking) or **weather stripping.**
3. Repeat the exercise near doorframes, electrical outlets, and other possible sources of air leaks.

Glossary

atmosphere the mixture of gases in contact with Earth's surface and extending far above.

atrium a large indoor space, usually with much vertical space.

biodegrade easily decomposed by living things.

blackwater used water flushed from toilets.

carbon dioxide a colorless, odorless gas given off by burning and by animals breathing out.

certification; certify to declare something true or correct by an official spoken, written, or printed statement; to provide certification.

clerestory window a window set in a roof or high in a wall that increases natural light.

compact fluorescent light bulb (CFL) a small fluorescent light bulb that screws into a standard light socket.

compost the process used to break down yard waste and food scraps into rich fertilizer for gardens and grass.

condensation the process of a gas changing into a liquid.

cool roof a roof that reflects the sun, reducing the need for artificial cooling.

cool tower a structure that uses the process of evaporation to cool air, which then circulates inside the building.

cooling load the amount of work that must be done to cool a building.

deforestation the destruction of forests.

desiccant a substance that attracts water and is thus capable of drawing water vapor out of air.

drywall a material for constructing walls, composed of gypsum backed with paper.

embodied energy the total amount of energy required to make a product or to carry out an activity.

emission an airborne waste product.

Energy Star a program run by the U.S. Environmental Protection Agency that rates energy and water efficiency of durable goods.

Environmental Protection Agency (EPA) the federal agency that works to protect the U.S. environment from pollution.

evaporate; evaporation to change from a liquid or solid into a vapor or gas; the act or process of changing a liquid or a solid into vapor.

fertilizer a substance that helps plants to grow.

fiberglass a material made of plastic embedded with glass fibers for strength.

fossil fuels underground deposits that were formed millions of years ago from the remains of plants and animals. Coal, oil, and natural gas are fossil fuels.

geothermal of, having to do with, or produced by action of the internal heat of the earth.

global warming the gradual warming of Earth's surface, believed to be caused by a build-up of greenhouse gases in the atmosphere.

graywater water that is not pure but is only moderately dirty; graywater can come from kitchen and shower drains or from rainwater.

green roof a roof that is covered with living plants.

greenhouse effect the process by which certain gases cause the Earth's atmosphere to warm.

greenhouse gas any gas that contributes to the greenhouse effect.

habitat the place where an animal or plant naturally lives or grows.

heat island effect the concentration of heat in areas densely packed with buildings, roads, and other human-made structures.

heavy metal a metal such as lead, mercury, and arsenic, which can collect in the tissues of organisms and is toxic to most living things.

incandescent light bulb a conventional light bulb that produces more heat than light.

insulation the quality of preventing heat from moving from one place to another.

landfill a place where trash and other solid waste materials are discarded.

light shelf a shelf placed on the outside area of a window to reflect sunlight back into the window.

light-emitting diode (LED) a tiny electrical device that generates light. LED's are highly energy efficient and give off little heat.

lightpipe a narrow reflective duct that channels daylight from a roof surface deeply into a building interior.

low-e window a window with a special metallic coating designed to block out direct rays of sunshine but to admit weaker, indirect rays.

mechanical refrigeration a technology for artificial cooling based on the scientific principles of evaporation and condensation.

nonpotable not clean enough to drink.

nonrenewable resources resources that cannot be replenished once depleted, such as fossil fuels.

permeable paving paving that allows rainwater to drain through it.

pesticide a poison that kills pests such as insects.

petroleum another name for the fossil fuel often called oil.

pollutant a single source of pollution.

power grid the interconnected system of power plants, transmission wires, and end-users of electricity.

radiant heating and cooling a system of temperature regulation that exchanges heat between an object (such as a floor) and the interior of a building.

rain garden a shallow depression in a landscape containing deep-rooted native plants, its purpose being to collect rainwater and allow it slowly to permeate the soil.

reclaimed; reclaiming saving old materials to use again in a similar way.

refrigerant the liquid used in a mechanical refrigeration system.

regulate; regulation to control by rule, principle, or system.

renewable resources natural resources, such as trees, that can be replaced after they have been harvested.

salvage; salvaging saving old materials to use in a similar way.

sewage water that contains waste matter produced by human beings.

solar cell a tiny device that converts the energy in sunlight to electric current.

solar panel a panel of solar cells.

solar power electricity that is created from the energy in sunlight.

solar reflectance the amount of sunlight that a surface reflects.

sustainable; sustainability any practice that adheres to principles of conservation and ecological balance.

synthetic material a manufactured material that does not exist in nature.

thermal chimney a hollow tower through which warm air exhausts out of a building.

thermal emittance the amount of heat that a warmed object radiates back.

thermal mass the ability to retain heat.

turbine a wheellike object that spins around and around.

United Nations an international organization that works for world peace and human prosperity.

ventilation exchanging inside air for outside air.

vinyl a type of plastic.

volatile organic compound (VOC) an unstable substance that breaks down over time and gives off small amounts of toxic gases.

weather stripping pieces of felt, foam rubber, or other bulky, insulating material used to stuff up cracks around doors and windows.

Additional Resources

WEB SITES

Turn to these Internet sources for more information on living green and the environment.

Building Green.com

http://www.buildinggreen.com

Publishes the online *Environmental Building News* and describes hundreds of building projects that support green technology.

Envirolink: Green Building Design

http://www.envirolink.org/topics.html?topic=Green%20Building%20Design&topicsku=2002119211137&topictype=subtopic

Provides access to over 100 online resources that deal with the design and construction of green buildings.

Green Building Initiative

http://www.thegbi.org/home.asp

A nonprofit organization that promotes both energy-efficient, healthy building practices for both homes and commercial buildings.

Healthy House Institute

http://www.healthyhouseinstitute.com

A source for articles on everything for the healthy home, from construction to interior furnishings.

Oikos

http://oikos.com/library/index.html

Contains a wealth of articles that describe green building techniques and devices, plus a "Green Building Glossary."

U.S. Department of Energy. Energy Efficiency and Renewable Energy

http://www.eere.energy.gov

Describes the various federal support programs for builders, including geothermal, solar, wind, and hydropower technologies.

U.S. Green Building Council

http://www.usgbc.org/DisplayPage.aspx?CategoryID=19

Presents information about the LEED rating system and certification.

BOOKS

Building Green
by Clarke Snell and Tim Callahan (Lark Books, 2005)

Green Building A to Z
by Jerry Yudelson (New Society, 2007)

The Green Building Revolution
by Jerry Yudelson (New Society, 2008)

Green from the Ground Up
by David Johnson and Scott Gobson (Taunton Press, 2008)

Greening Your Home
by Clayton Bennett (McGraw-Hill, 2008)

Your Green Home
by Alex T. Wilson (New Society, 2006)

Index